YOUR TOOTH IS KILLING ME

The balance between the clinical aspect of
dentistry and the business of dentistry

KEVIN COUGHLIN DMD

ISBN 10: 1508450307
ISBN 13: 9781508450306

I dedicate these thoughts—

- To my mom and dad, Mr. Ralph Coughlin and Mrs. Joyce Coughlin, the two greatest teachers that anyone could ever have;
- To my brother, Dr. Bret Coughlin, the hardest worker and smartest individual I have ever come across;
- To my wife, Karen, who has shown incredible support to me over the years;
- To my three children, Jared, Taylor, and Shayla, who show me every day that the greatest investment is in human capital; I am proud of you each and every day.

I would like to also give personal thanks to Mr. Peter Stabile and Dr. Lewis Rigali who took the time and energy to introduce me to the field of dentistry and the business and clinical aspects of dentistry. Perhaps more importantly, they showed me what a tremendous impact another individual can have on someone by taking the time to teach, explain, and show the wonderful opportunities that are available in the fields of medicine and dentistry.

CONTENTS

INTRODUCTION

IT HAS BECOME increasingly clear each year that there are many professionals, particularly in my area of expertise (dentistry), who need guidance. I have given numerous seminars and provided hundreds, if not thousands, of hours of continuing education in the field of clinical dentistry and in the business of dentistry. The questions I receive are almost always the same. I have been answering phone calls and emails almost every evening from dental students, professionals who are just getting started, as well as seasoned dentists who are asking how they can build their dental practices. I have been asked over numerous occasions to try to put my thoughts and recommendations into book form to help guide dental professionals through a journey that, like most journeys, has peaks and valleys. Nothing in this book is really original. I wish it was. Everything I say or write, I have learned from someone else. What I hope to accomplish is to guide you in the organization of these thoughts in a way to make your journey more fun and profitable. When I can remember who told me something or taught me something, or I read something, I will try to give credit. I hope this book will make your journey enjoyable and provide you with more time and money to enjoy your life and help others enjoy theirs.

1

Background

THE BEST WAY to start is to share briefly a list of some of my common principles. Select the correct type of dental office. Select a location you are willing to live and practice in for the long term. Make sure that the person you decide on practicing with, you believe in, like, and trust. Do not waste time. If a change is necessary do not take too much time to make that change. Remember the fewer the changes; the better off you will be. Try to make your first job your last job. Learn to communicate better. Learn to sell yourself, your care, and your services. Learn to become a better leader. Throughout this book, I will provide information that you can use, as you would the information from any textbook, to guide you through the maze of making better decisions and fewer poor decisions. At the top of the list is this: understand that your most important asset is time.

Consider your business career and job searching very much like developing a relationship. Think for a moment of the cost, time, stress, and energy wasted by picking the wrong partner. Now imagine the cost, time, stress, and energy used, when that first job does not work out, or the long -term employment fails, or partnership does not occur. What a mess...Of course, bad things happen, and sometimes they cannot be helped; but take the appropriate steps to increase your odds for success. Consider the following: (which can apply to both your business and personal life). First, understand the different parties involved, such as other associates, staff members, owners, and their partners or spouses. Each group has different wants and needs, be aware of this. Ask the following questions: What is the track record for each group when it comes to relationships? How many associates has the practice had? Why did the associate leave? In most cases the associate will not be happy with his or her job because they are not practicing the dentistry they intended. Second, the associate and or significant other wants to live in another area, perhaps closer to family and friends. Third, the associate is changing jobs due to marriage issues or divorce. Fourth, they may only want to work part-time. Keep in mind that according to some statistics, 80% of all associateships fail within the first two years. Other reasons partnerships fail could be that the associate has little experience, or the owner doing the hiring has little experience. So, in many cases, we have the blind leading the blind. The owner is certainly not without fault. In many cases the owner does not have enough internal controls to monitor and mentor. The owner does not have the proper infrastructure such as staff, software, space, and equipment. Many times the owner miscalculates their patient base and will not have enough patients to keep both parties happy. In the end, the single biggest reason for failure, in my opinion, is that both parties do not truly believe, like, and trust in each other--what I call the BLT. Be sure you both have enough BLT before you establish the relationship. A successful business arrangement or partnership, has a lot in common with a successful personal relationship. In most successful relationships you need trust, honesty, integrity, and financial security. The more information you have before going into a relationship, personal or business, the greater the likelihood of success.

If at all possible, try to choose the correct job in the correct location right at the start. Over my many years of interviewing dental associates, the common theme I have found is that they have worked at three or more associate positions and, in my opinion, wasted valuable time and enormous amounts of money by doing so. How you find that right job is similar to finding the right spouse. Many of the attributes you use in connecting into a relationship you should consider using in finding the right job and location. If you are only interested in a short-term relationship, then your approach will be much different than if you are looking for a long-term relationship. Most people, if they are honest, will tell you that a successful long-term relationship is much better and surely less stressful than a short-term relationship, and in most cases better financially. Do your homework, evaluate what you want and do not want, and then create a plan and follow that plan. Understand that, like most plans, it will change along with your wants and needs. There is no problem with change; it is part of life. Remember a job opportunity that offers significantly more money may not be the correct option. Most dentists do not want to see a patient every 15-20 minutes and only do restorations and prophies. If the offer seems too good to be true, perhaps it is not the correct decision. However, keep in mind that everything that feels good is not necessarily good for you! In the end, use your head AND listen to your gut.

Set aside a certain amount of money each month with the goal to have enough financial stability so that you can work the rest of your life only because you want to, not because you have to. Remember, nobody knows everything. Seek experts in your personal and business career.

Also remember that there are three types of capital: human capital, intellectual capital, and financial capital. I believe that human capital is the most important.

A successful life is a life that is balanced. I am a graduate of Springfield College in Springfield, Massachusetts, whose motto declares that in order to have true success you must build your "mind, body, and spirit." Keeping a balance in your personal life, business life, and spiritual life, will most likely provide you with the best long-term success and the most happiness.

2

LET'S GET TO WORK

WHY DO I think that I have the knowledge to write a book to help our dental profession? I started my first general dental office right after graduation from Tufts School of Dental Medicine in 1983, completely and totally unprepared for the business world and, completely unprepared for the clinical aspects of dentistry. Currently, my dental practice has grown to fourteen dental offices, approximately one hundred and fifty full- and part-time employees, and, there is almost nothing that could happen in business or in the clinical field of dentistry that I have not experienced firsthand. Consider the following:

"Dr. Coughlin, Mr. Smith is upset that his filling feels high."

"Dr. Coughlin, Ms. Smith is upset that her tooth is sensitive after the filling."

"Dr. Coughlin, Mr. Smith did not realize that he was going to be out of network, and he doesn't feel he should be responsible for any costs of treatment."

"Dr. Coughlin, Ms. Smith has been waiting for over one hour for her dental appointment; she is very upset and does not want to return to our office."

"Dr. Coughlin, Mr. Smith went to the wrong location, and we forgot to confirm him for the correct office."

"Dr. Coughlin, Ms. Smith has a broken tooth that was left in her jaw after an extraction."

"Dr. Coughlin, Mr. Smith is upset because he feels the wrong tooth was treated."

"Dr. Coughlin, Ms. Smith says her implant is loose."

"Dr. Coughlin, ever since Mr. Smith had his tooth removed, his TMJ has been hurting, and he is unable to open correctly."

"Dr. Coughlin, Ms. Smith feels that her child has been treated inappropriately."

"Dr. Coughlin, Mr. Smith feels that the doctor is on some kind of medication because he or she is not acting right."

"Dr. Coughlin, an attorney is on the line and would like to talk to you about his or her client who is upset with care and service."

"Dr. Coughlin, someone from the licensing board is on the phone and needs to speak to you immediately about a patient who has registered a complaint and is unhappy with care and service."

"Dr. Coughlin, Dr. Coughlin, Dr. Coughlin." The point I'm trying to make in this book is that I have a lot of practical experience, along with a Master's degree in business. With a patient base of over thirty thousand and more than eighty thousand patient visits per year, I feel I have some experience. One thing should be obvious: I do not like what I am hearing from Mr. or Ms. Smith!

The above issues are the result of proper procedures and processes not being followed. You might think, therefore, that perhaps we do not have proper training manuals or videos available or spend enough time on training, mentoring, coaching, teaching, or additional continuing education courses. This not the case, however.

We meet at least every month for two to three hours for clinical and business training with our dental associates, hygienists, dental assistants, IT people, IS people, front desk coordinators, managers, regional managers, and core group. What's missing is a failure to follow proper procedures and processes, which may lead to mistakes. A solution to these problems would be to have someone with strong, dynamic leadership abilities, as well as business and clinical expertise, in each and every facility. I refer to this type of person as the "boots on the ground" who will make sure all processes and procedures are followed precisely to a "T". I strongly recommend that when you interview for your new job, be certain to ensure proper procedures and processes are in place and being followed at your prospective place of employment.

I could list many examples of mistakes from more than thirty years of stress, aggravation, and disappointment, but it would accomplish little to nothing. I accept my position and my responsibility along with the decisions I have made. It is my job to improve our service, reduce our mistakes, and create an organization that is truly great. Reaching our goal is really made up of many steps in a process that never ends. It really is the journey and not the destination that makes us who we are.

3

How to Start Off Right

IN ORDER TO find the right job, you first have to decide what you are looking for. Would you like a career in academics? Would you like to pursue public health? Would you like to consider specialty care? Would you like to consider a general dental residency? Would you like to just start out practicing in the field of dentistry right from graduation from dental school? Once that decision is made, it will be time to change your focus to the next area of career development.

My focus in this book will be dedicated to the vast majority of you who are electing to go directly into dental practice. In my opinion, the following suggestions and recommendations will apply to you whether you go into a specialty practice or a general dental practice.

The next decision that must be addressed is whether you would prefer to work in the city, the country, or the suburbs. You then must decide whether you would like to work as a solo practitioner, in a small group practice, or in a large group practice. In many cases, you will be unsure. What makes the most sense for you as an individual depends in a large part on the type of personality you have and the wants and needs you have. Some example questions you may want to ask yourself are:

1. Do you prefer to hire your own employees?
2. Do you enjoy networking and meetings?
3. Do you have a clear and unique vision of the type of dental practice you want?

4. Are you comfortable developing policies and procdures on a wide varity of topics?
5. Are you passionate about creating your own professional environment and surroundings?
6. Are you willing to invest the time it takes to get started?
7. Are you comfortable being financially frugal for a time?
8. Are you comfortable creating your own patient base?
9. Are you comfortable selecting your own equipment?
10. Are you excited about becoming an entrepreneur and creating a new business?
11. Do you feel you have the skills to sell yourself and your business?
12. Can you be flexible with your location and community?
13. Do you care about having a connection with your community?

If you answered "yes" to the above questions, then you may want to consider starting your own dental practice.

Also consider these questions:
1. Would you prefer to inherit a base of employees?
2. Would you prefer to rely on internal referrals from an existing patient base?
3. Do you think you can find an acceptable dental practice that meets your wants and needs?
4. Do you think you can adapt to policies and procedures that are already in place?
5. Would you prefer to work in a previously established office environment?
6. Do you want to hit the ground running with no time to spare?
7. Do you want immediate cash flow?
8. Do you feel you need to have an already established patient base?
9. Are you comfortable allowing someone else to select your equipment?
10. Are you uncomfortable with sales?

If you answered "yes" to these questions, then you may want to consider a practice acquisition.

Always remember that either option can be successful. The key is looking inward into what works best for your particular wants and needs.

Remember that those wants and needs can change over time, so do not hesitate to make those changes. However, the fewer changes made, the less time wasted; the sooner you will achieve your goals and reach financial stability.

Once you have decided where you want to work, the questions become: What type of environment would you like to work in? How should you seek out job opportunities? How do you find these opportunities? To state the obvious, an excellent place to start is to tap into the alumni networks of the dental school from which you graduated. If your school does not have an alumni network, I strongly recommend that you start one.

Another wonderful source for job opportunities is the salespeople who work for dental supply facilities (such as Patterson Dental, Henry Schein, and Benco). There are certainly many more supply companies that have contacts and networks with literally tens of thousands of dentists all across the United States and the world. These salespeople are intimately associated with the workings of the practices that they call on day after day. They are a great and free resource because they know who may be looking for an associate.

Another job search option is to consider headhunters or placement companies. These are firms, like dating services, that take your data and match you up with "like individuals." In most cases, these headhunting services will not charge you a fee. Rather, they charge the fee to your future employer upon hire. Using a placement company can often save you time, energy, and money. An example of one of these firms is the Patterson Placement Service, www.etsdental.com at 1-540-491-9118. There are many other firms that will be happy to help you.

The use of the internet or the Yellow Pages can also aid in a job search. Select a group of dentists from that source, then call or send a letter asking if there is an opening. If so, request an interview. No one option is better than another, but your personality, your financial situation, and your time commitment may influence your selection. Do not forget that another job search source may be the dentist who has been providing care to you and your family. Even if you are not interested in returning to that location with that particular practice, that dentist may be an excellent source of information and guidance and may provide connections with dentists all over the world.

Of course, to pursue these opportunities, you will need a curriculum vitae (CV) to express your interests and your goals. After evaluating thousands of CVs, my personal opinion is that most new graduates look exactly the same on paper. In most cases, you lack experience, but you are looking to be hired. If at all possible in your CV try to demonstrate characteristic of drive, determination, maturity, and sincerity. The ability to stay at one location for a long period of time is an asset. In my practice, for example, I would be interested in hiring someone who would plan on staying two years or longer.

Try to look at things from two perspectives. One is the new dentist looking to be hired, while the other is the dentist who will be doing the hiring. The process of finding a job should take time and energy on both parties. I cannot stress enough how expensive, time-consuming, and draining hiring any employee can be; particularly in hiring a dental associate--only to find that he or she wants another type of location or practice.

Step 1. I strongly recommend that you start your search with a phone interview. That phone interview is usually best done after hours when you both have time and are relaxed. During this phone interview, you should be asking what the dentist is looking for in an associate. Is he or she looking for a long-term relationship or a short-term one? Is he or she looking to sell the practice and, if so, over what time frame. Try to understand the dentist's overall philosophy on how he or she practices and markets the practice. What is the dentist's vision for the practice? Would you be an employee or the future owner of that business?

These are extremely important points of information to gather and ponder during the phone conversation. There is no right or wrong. You just need to make the best decision that will lead to a successful outcome for both parties.

Step 2. If after the phone interview both parties feel there is an interest, I would strongly recommend that you visit the practice. During that visit you should have the following prepared questions:

What are the office hours?

Do you provide care on weekends and evenings?

Do you provide early morning office hours?

Do you close during lunch?

How do you schedule?

Is the associate on production or collection?

Which procedures are done and approximately how many procedures are done within that schedule?

If the practice does 90 percent implant surgery, and you have no implant interest, perhaps that would be a red flag that this practice may not be the appropriate for you. Conversely, if the practice sees only hygiene patients and exams, but otherwise refers almost everything out (like molar root canals, surgical extractions, periodontal surgical procedures, TMJ, and orthodontics), while your interest is in providing care and service in these areas, then in most cases this would not be the correct practice for you.

During this interview, it is important that you evaluate the size of the practice in terms of square feet and number of operatories. Does the practice have only three operatories within 1,000 square feet? You might ask where you would practice, especially if those three operatories where occupied by one doctor, one associate, and one hygienist for the office. In such a situation, there would be no room for you, and it is very unlikely that you will receive any mentoring. I think it is critically important that the practice has at least four operatories and at least 2,500 square feet to accommodate an average size dental practice providing care for 1,200-1,800 active patients.

You will also want to know the following:

Will the facility need upgrades?

Does the office have a consultation room?

Is the business office private so that patients in the reception room do not hear what is going on at the front desk?

Does the property have room for expansion?

Is the property owned or leased?

If it is leased, what are the terms?

What are the general conditions or market conditions of the surrounding city, town, or suburban area?

Is the area growing or is it shrinking?

What is the average income of the family in that area?

What is the average educational background of the people living in the area, how many people have a college degree or higher?

How many dentists are practicing in the area as general dentists?

How many specialists are in the area?

By the way, all of the demographics can be ascertained through the internet. The problem that many of us have is not knowing how to interpret the data. As a general rule, I believe that a dentist needs at least two thousand active patients to make his or her practice successful. An active patient is an individual who comes in at least every eighteen months.

As part of the interview, I also feel you should meet with the staff including the front desk coordinator, the dental hygienists, and the dental assistants. Evaluate the processes and procedures, how they handle informed consents and financial arrangements, and how they sterilize and clean instruments. Evaluate their supplies—how many instruments do they have? Ask whether you would have your own full-time dental assistant, or whether you would be sharing an assistant with the senior dentist. Will that senior dentist be present while you are practicing, or will that dentist be off-site? Clearly, if the dentist is off-site, there will be very little mentoring and very little opportunity for you to be helped. If you are just getting started in your career, write down these points and check them off one by one to make sure that you have addressed each and every one of these issues.

Step 3. Once the interview is complete, I strongly recommend, if time is available, that you meet with this dentist or group during off-hours. Whether it is for lunch or dinner, it is important to get out of the dental setting and into a social setting to get an idea of that dentist's personality and family. Consider the dynamics of his or her family if you have the opportunity. In many cases, the dentist's business is a mirror image of the family. A fragmented and dysfunctional family many times leads to a fractured and dysfunctional dental practice.

Step 4. Once this information is acquired and digested the next issue is to get hard facts about the practice. The following are some suggestions:

Will you be the first dental associate, or will you be one of many? If the doctor had associates in the past, and they are still present, this is usually a good sign. If an associate moved on, find out why.

You should also understand:

- What duties you will be performing?
- What hours you will be working?
- What type of care you will be providing?

- How you will be compensated for those services?
- What duration of time you will be providing these services?

You should have a definitive start date, and you should be comfortable with the employment contract that you will be signing. In my opinion, it is critical that you have a written contract or employment agreement so that there are no misunderstandings.

Step 5. The next issue is deciding what the compensation package will be. As a general rule, you will be paid either on straight production, straight collection, a salary, or some combination of the above. In fact, some associates are simply paid a daily rate. I strongly urge someone who is new to a dental practice to consider a combination of a guaranteed salary and a commission. I say this for several reasons. In most cases, if you are a new dentist in a new setting, you will not be familiar with the staff or the client base, so it will take time to generate what I refer to as the BLT—believe, like, and trust. It normally takes some period of time for the staff, the senior doctor, and patient base to get to know you.

When just getting started, even as an associate, you should definitely know what your expense structure is. It is hard enough to guess what your income will be, especially when most newcomers will underestimate their expenses. The flipside of the coin is that being an employer can be more risky, so many times it is difficult for the senior doctor to guarantee a salary for the new doctor whose skills and experience are unknown. Some general suggestions are as follows:

Between 28 percent and 40 percent of production or collection seems to be reasonable as an expected income. At present, I think it is reasonable to expect a starting salary of $100,000 or more based on the practice, patient base, and your ability to perform dental care and service. As a general rule, I use the multiple of three to five. That simply means, if I am going to pay someone $100,000, I would like to see that person be able to collect between $300,000 and $500,000. A dental hygienist who earns $40 an hour should collect and produce between $120 and $200 an hour.

It is important that we discuss the issue of production as related to earnings. In many cases, a new dentist will be unclear of how much he or she will produce. It appears to me that the average graduating dental student has been seeing between two and four patients a day. Thus, in most cases, newly graduated associate's ability to produce is significantly reduced because of a lack of experience and speed. This situation creates a problem because you may be forced to work faster doing things that you may not yet have experience doing at this point in your career. My point is that you should be realistic; understand that in most cases your employer will want to make some kind of profit after he or she has paid overhead and your salary and/ or commission.

Step 6. The next issue to discuss, after the salary and commission, is the benefits. The list of benefits that should be addressed includes:

- time off
- sick and personal time
- vacation time
- medical insurance
- life insurance
- disability insurance
- malpractice insurance
- continuing education
- time off for continuing education
- savings plans (whether they be pension plans, a 401(k), or other types of vehicles)

In addition, signing bonuses, transportation costs, and relocation costs all make up a vast array of benefits. Obviously, some benefits may be more important than others as you negotiate your employment contract. Clearly, the more you get the better off you may be. Keep in mind that, if the benefit package sounds too good, a red flag should go up because most employers cannot afford to lose money on any employee. Consequently, you should evaluate the practice to determine what the benefits are for the other employees. In some cases more long-term employees will have additional benefits or perhaps better benefits. This can give you a picture of what your future may be like.

Step 7. Once you have established the benefits package and a compensation package that you are comfortable with, you should review the package so that you understand it. In addition, I would strongly recommend that someone who is knowledgeable in the dental profession evaluate the contract with you for your own protection.

Another important part of this employee contract should address certain key points such as restrictive covenants. A restrictive covenant means, that you are generally asked upon termination to "not compete" or open a practice during a certain period of time in a certain geographic area. This stipulation is based on particular state laws, and the density of the population. As a general rule, a five-to-seven-mile distance from an office for a period of 12 to 24 months would seem reasonable for both parties. The employer is trying to protect his or her patient base and business. Yet, from the employee standpoint, you should not be restricted unnecessarily from providing the care and services you would like to provide in any area where you would like to practice. My personal opinion is that staff and patients will gravitate to the people and places where they are most comfortable.

Some further points to review:

- Do everything you can do to make your first job be your last job. This will avoid wasted time, which means wasted money.
- Do your due diligence to make sure you are comfortable with the location of the practice, the type of practice, and the duties that you will be performing in that practice.
- Make sure that the practice has a patient base large enough to support your care and services. This is usually twelve hundred to two thousand active patients per doctor.
- Make sure that the demographics of that patient base suit your particular wants and needs whether that is cultural, financial, educational, or any other combination. You will best evaluate this base by evaluating the average age of the patients, the type of insurances that are accepted by the practice, the types of procedures, and the number of procedures that are done on a yearly basis in the practice. For example, if the practice has very few children in it, in most cases you will provide very little orthodontics. Or if the practice has a very high population of government assistance programs, you will most likely provide very low percentage of crown and bridge procedures.

- Remember to evaluate the profile of the community you are working in, as well as the profile of the staff and dentist with whom you will be working.
- Remember that by preparing for the interview with proper diligence, you will get a fairly good idea of what you can expect in your future position.

4

THE NEGOTIATION

YOU THINK YOU found the location and type of practice that interests you. You have done your due diligence, and so the next step is to negotiate a fair compensation package.

Keep in mind that with any agreement, that if it is too "one-sided" it will always fail. If you think you are getting rich quick, chances are the long-term success of this relationship is guarded at best. A compensation package, to work long-term and to provide the best outcome, has to accommodate all parties involved. This is no different with your professional service agreement, which should generally be considered as a contract between you and your employer. I would strongly advise that a professional service agreement be drawn up and evaluated by an attorney who represents you and has knowledge about the fields of dentistry and medicine. Personally, I believe this professional service agreement should be a contract for at least 12 months, and my recommendation would be 24 months. The most important points in any contract or agreement are the duties and responsibilities for the new hire, as well as that person's qualifications and the maintenance of those qualifications within the time period specified in the contract. Those qualifications include:

- maintaining an unrestricted license
- being able to perform professional services
- maintaining skills

- abiding by the principles and ethics of the American Dental Association
- complying with all federal, state, and municipal laws
- maintaining appropriate and accurate dental records

The compensation and benefits described in the agreement are as follows. The agreement should make sure that the dentist is eligible to participate in third-party payments. The agreement should also address the consequences if the dentist is convicted of a criminal offense. In addition, the agreement should outline procedures and processes when determining the billing assignment and delivery of revenues. In most cases your employment will involve you providing dental services on patients who have some type of dental insurance. These insurance companies, in many cases, will direct patients to your care since you will be listed on their web page as a provider. The first step will be to make sure you have been credentialed. You will need to fill out and sign a contract with these insurance companies. These companies will want to know if you have any pending litigation or past law suits, or even any discplinary actions with State Boards. They will want to make sure your licenses are in order and in good standing. They will want to make sure your continuing education is also up to date. Please remember, if you are not credentialed you will not be able to treat those patients, and you will not be able to bill those insurance companies. In many cases, credentialing can take several weeks to complete and should be addressed as soon as the employment contract is signed.

As you review your professional contract or service agreement, consider that there are some primary items that most service agreements should contain. The following is a description of those items and what they mean. There should be:

- a notice of engagement, which simply means the parties are getting together
- a designated term (a time period for your employment)
- a list of duties and responsibilities that are expected of the new dentist. (These requirements should be clear to make sure that there are no misunderstandings, for example, whether or not the

new dentist will be "on call" and whether or not he or she will be compensated for being "on call")

- a list of the new dentist's qualifications
- a requirement that the new dentist will maintain his or her license in the standards spelled out for that particular state

Make sure there are no restrictions to your DEA license, state boards, and malpractice insurances. Anyone of these issues will prevent you from performing your duties as a new hire. It is imperative that you:

- maintain a Drug Enforcement Administration certificate
- maintain your skills
- abide by the principles and ethics of the American Dental Association
- comply with all federal, state, and municipal laws, statutes, ordinances, and other regulations
- understand the guidelines adopted by the company or individual that you will be working with
- maintain appropriate and accurate dental records in accordance with accepted standards

In the agreement, there should also be:

- notes regarding outside interests or conflict of interest
- a list of compensation and benefits with exhibits explaining how these compensations and benefits will be carried out
- notes on the dentist's eligibility to participate in insurance plans
- notes on what happens should the dentist be convicted of a criminal offense
- notes on what occurs if the dentist should lose his or her license or its suspension
- notes on whether the dentist's license has any restrictions
- Questions that should be answered in the agreement include:
- how billing assignment and delivery of revenue will proceed
- how to handle termination for cause by the employer or by the employee

- what happens upon immediate termination
- what happens upon termination without cause
- what will occur upon death or disability
- how to handle the resolution of disputes
- what to do for withholding and tax purposes
- how patient records should be handled
- what are the restrictions in your non-compete clause
- how to handle confidentiality of patient and employee information (remember that you are an employee of this facility, and in most cases, the information should be kept confidential and is the owner's property)
- how long would you be restricted from practicing in the area, should you set up your own office
- what the consequences would be for soliciting patients or staff members from that practice, should you go your separate ways
- how these covenants should be enforced and for what period of time
- what penalties would be enforced if the agreement was not followed what happens to the accounts receivables if you leave or your contract expires

Also, there should be a discussion of malpractice in terms naming who is responsible for paying the premiums, as well as how it should be maintained and at what level. Are you paying the premiums or is the owner? In most cases dental malpractice will be either a claims-made policy or occurrence policy. In the claims-made type of malpractice insurance, after you stop practicing dentistry (for whatever reason) the malpractice coverage stops. This is usually less expensive, but a higher risk to the dentist. The other option is called an occurrence plan. This type of plan stays in effect even after you stop practicing dentistry. This plan is usually more expensive, but provides a higher level of protection. Further, there should be a discussion of barter and courtesy—how much latitude do you have or do not have in giving professional courtesies or discounts?

All of these particular issues should be in your service agreement or contract. Please review them with the appropriate legal professional who has a background in the fields of medicine and dentistry.

The next important consideration for most dentists signing the professional agreement is the compensation package and benefits. As far as benefits go, you would look at malpractice, medical, dental, life, and disability insurance; continuing education; licensing; fees for journal and magazine subscriptions affiliated with your profession; personal and sick leave and vacation time. Along with all this, you may want to ask if there is any type of pension or 401(k) plan that would allow you to start saving immediately.

My opinion, after years of experience in this field, is that generally you, the new dentist, will not be familiar with the community or area and will not have a patient base. The pressures of paying your own personal bills, maintaining an adequate lifestyle, and paying your educational and personal debt can many times put outside pressures on you. Therefore, compensation in the form of just collection or production may put the emphasis more on doing and less on the quality of care in the service you will be providing. As a result, I personally believe that a combination of a guaranteed salary along with an incentive package will make the most sense.

There is no exact science in negotiating any compensation package, but there are some general rules to consider that might help you. First, before you go into the negotiation, understand what your debt is and what your net income will be. Net income simply means the net number you are left with after you have paid your federal, state, and social security taxes, which can be anywhere from 28 to 40 percent of your gross income. I suggest that, before you start to negotiate, you know what your budget is. Keep in mind that before you start your negotiations, you consider what net income will be necessary to pay your fixed expenses as well as hidden expenses. So if you make $100,000, chances are you will be bringing home $70,000 or less after taxes. Out of that $70,000 take home income, you have to budget for fixed expenses such as rent or a mortgage, transportation, education loans, clothing, entertainment, food, and miscellaneous expenses. Know what your expenses are and write them down. You should know that you need more income than you think just to make ends meet.

There are also hidden expenses. Some of these hidden expenses that you should consider are:
- other taxes, including any excise, property, or sales taxes
- transportation costs including car maintenance, parking, public transportation
- maintenance of a house, apartment, condominium and fees associated with those types of housing arrangements
- malpractice, disability, life, medical, dental, and car insurance
- education loan debt
- entertainment
- clothing
- savings or investments
- charitable contributions
- food
- vacation travel

You can see quickly that the expenses add up. There is almost no end to the list. Perhaps the most important item in this list, in my personal opinion, is savings or investments. I recommend, no matter how difficult it is, that you automatically set aside some amount of money each month that will go into a savings account. As a general rule as you get started, strive to save 10 percent of your net earnings. If you can save more, you will be rewarded significantly as the years march on due to the time value of money and the discipline of starting a savings account while you are young.

Once you know what your debt is, and you have estimated what you need to live on, it is then time to negotiate your compensation package. Again, the combination of a guaranteed salary and some kind of incentive bonus appears to make the most sense to me. The higher risk is with the employer because the employer has to guarantee something. However, to provide a high level of care and services and to protect the practice's reputation, I believe this combination is best. Whether you are a seasoned dentist who has just relocated, or you are a new graduate with a residency program behind you, you are still new to that practice and a risk to your employer. If you have just graduated from school, your lack of experience can have an effect on that guaranteed salary. I think that the amount of training, effort, time, and money invested in your training justifies a six-figure salary. However, your skills, your speed, and what that practice can produce may often put restrictions on the amount that you will earn.

I am a big believer in a graduated salary and compensation based on incentives for the first twelve to twenty-four months. For example:

between $6,000 and $11,000 per month for the first four months
between $8,000 and $13,000 per month for the next four months
between $10,000 and $14,000 per month for the next four months.

This graduated salary would be a base salary that you would be guaranteed, providing you abide by the service agreement that you signed. In other words, you perform the duties that are expected—be at work on time, be responsible for your duties, and provide a high level of care and service for your patients— and your salary will not depend on production or collection. In addition, in the 12 to 24 months, you will receive an incentive if you net collect or net produce a certain amount every quarter. The reason for this incentive is to encourage and reward excellence in performance. The added incentive to stay and provide a high level of service and care is greatly appreciated and rewarded.

When there is an incentive bonus, I believe that both parties benefit. Obviously, both parties have to be respectful so as not to take advantage of any incentive program. As a new dentist, you must understand that, when you stay after hours, there is a higher risk not only to the patient but also to yourself and to the practice that is employing you. In most cases when staying late, you will not have a full support staff, so if problems occur, chances are the outcome will be less than ideal. Also, you have to understand that there are additional costs. Those employees who are staying create an increase in overhead. The heat, the electricity, and such all have additional costs that will have to be paid by the owner and that practice. You must be aware that most employees do not mind staying late or helping, but they don't want such events to occur day after day because your staff will find it an inconvenience. They also have lives and commitments after work.

What kind of compensation can vary? Compensation does not necessarily have to be monetary. It could be benefits such as additional time off or additional continuing education, but in most cases both parties will agree on some kind of financial incentive. That incentive, in my opinion, should be a percentage of profit, and that percentage can be anywhere from 5 to 33 percent. There comes a point in the very beginning of your career when you have to make a decision. That decision is whether you are going to stay an employee and, if so, whether you are willing to become a long-term employee. This situation would mean that you are willing to sign a contract or another service agreement for three years or longer. Keep in mind that there is no negative to this choice, and in many cases, this may be an appropriate vehicle for you to pursue if you are not interested in owning your own practice.

Another option that you will have to consider, if you are not interested in being a long-term employee, is whether you would be interested in buying the entire practice or some portion of that practice. This action would, or could, lead to partnership. If you elect the latter, where you will become a full and equal partner, you might ultimately take over the entire company. I strongly recommend that you consider a test run for 6 to 12 months prior to signing the final agreement. What I mean by a test run is that for the first 12 to 24 months, you've been guaranteed a salary, and you generally have not been associated with any debt or any experience in running the practice for other dentists. For those who would like to pursue this particular route of ownership, I strongly recommend you change your contract and get paid a percentage of your collections. Then you become responsible for overseeing and running the dental practice along with overhead and laboratory fees. This situation will be an excellent lesson that forces you to look clearly into what the future of ownership may entail.

After decades of experience working with dental associates in multiple offices, I have found that most dentists are totally divorced from the business side of the equation. The cost of running a business is not only financial, but also involves the time commitment associated with running a successful business. Some of the intangibles that I would like to address are the time it takes to:

- hire and fire
- interview
- evaluate reports
- process payroll
- pay bills
- meet with suppliers, contractors, and staff
- provide and participate in continuing education
- ensure compliance with such regulations as HIPPA and OSHA

- deal with patient problems
- handle insurance issues such as which insurance to accept
- develop a budget
- determine and evaluate a marketing plan
- review profit and loss through income statements and balance sheets

All of these are tangible items that take time and cost money. In most cases, the associate is not only inexperienced in these areas, but also he or she generally has no idea about the amount of time and money it takes to evaluate these particular areas. If the practice that you are associated with is a large dental practice, many times there will be a layer of employees or consultants to take care of these tasks. That extra layer of staff also has an effect on overhead. However, at some point the owner has a fiduciary responsibility to evaluate and verify that the tasks and procedures and processes are done properly. Ultimately, as the owner, you are the responsible party-- "Trust, but verify."

For those doctors considering some type of partnership or ownership, I suggest that in the 6 to 12 months prior to making a final decision, they base their income on a percentage of collection. A figure between 28 and 40 percent of collection seems equitable as a base income. Included in overhead expenes should be a percentage, if not 100 percent, of the laboratory bills associated with their production. They should then be brought into the loop to evaluate what is necessary and expected in running a successful business.

At the end of 6 to 12 months, both parties will have a very clear understanding as to whether this partnership will be successful long term or not. In many cases, the heart is in the right place, but the wallet is not. In some cases, the overhead for that practice may be high, and that overhead will have to be trimmed down or the associate will have to be more productive if the partnership is to be successful. In some instances, the associate's skills (whether clinical, communication, business, or a combination of all three) may not have reached the point of experience where he or she can handle the pressure, the debt structure, and the overhead structure of running a business. In this case, the partnership should be postponed in the best interest of the company, the owner, and the associate.

5

LET THE FUN BEGIN

YOU HAVE NOW been hired, and you are about to start your first job. Let the fun begin.

I would like for you to consider following ten basic principles:

1. Having a vision
2. Holding to a code of conduct
3. Communicating relentlessly
4. Planning financially
5. Raising the bar
6. Becoming a final decision maker
7. Soliciting help and support
8. Demanding excellence
9. Implementing and using technology
10. Facilitating continuous positive action

Remember to be patient; all good things take time. Follow these ten principles, to help you succeed in your business and personal careers. What we are actually discussing is your leadership skills. You are no longer a student at a university. You are taking the steps in becoming a true professional, not only in the crafts of dentistry and medicine, but also in the art of business and in the development of your profile to become a successful leader. This last item can mean many things, but make no mistake—you are the leader, and success will either occur or not based on your leadership skills.

I recommend that you consider the following skills. These skills can be learned; however, they may come to some individuals easier than others. These skills may also apply to the owner that your working with; this is an important concept to understand. An individual may own the dental practice and be in the process of hiring you, but they may not possess all these leadership skills as dentist and/or owner, actually, very few will.

There are many characteristics of a good leader, but the following are fairly all encompassing. They are: vision, tolerance, trust, attitude, motivation, purpose, awareness, determination, tenacity, inspiration, commitment, self-control, endeavor, faith, willpower, and patience. If you can focus on these factors, along with improving your strengths and reducing your weaknesses in each of these areas, your journey will truly be successful. The new dentist can benefit from this section, as well as the seasoned dentist. Can anyone argue, that we can all improve and should improve our leadership skills?

Vision means to teach or understand what your ideal future can be--this includes your values. Remember that what you want your organization to be may not be the vision the people around you have in mind. The sooner you can get your team's vision in sync with your vision, the easier this journey to success will be.

Tolerance means to respect others views. Do not sell yourself short, but try to understand the perspective of others and realize they may not understand your vision for the practice.

Trust is necessary to create the correct environment in your organization. Remember trust is part of the triangle BLT, which stands for believe, like, and trust. In all cases, trust must be earned.

Attitude is a small thing that can make an enormous difference. Your employees will feed off your positive energy. Negative energy will bring down not only yourself, but also your organization.

Motivation is a huge key to success. Remember that what motivates one person may not motivate another. Find the switch and learn how to use that switch. In most cases, key motivating factors for patients will be fear, money, and time. I should also include the motivation of ego. Most people, young or old, want to feel good about themselves and their appearance.

Purpose is what should be driving every aspect of your business. In my case, the purpose of our dental organization is to be so good at what we do, that our patients are anxious to tell their family and friends about our dental practice and the care and service they receive. What is the purpose of your business? The sooner you can align all your employees and your patients to follow your business plan, the sooner you will achieve your financial goals.

Awareness is a personal understanding of your identity and that of the people around you. It is the very core of one's identity. You must be constantly aware of the feelings and emotions of your staff, your patients, and your family.

Determination is a trait you must posess if you want to become a leader. You must never allow your determination to take a vacation. It should never get sick, and it has to be working every day. Determination, in my opinion, is one of the most important characteristics of a leader.

Tenacity means that, no matter what the challenge, you will never ever give up!

Inspiration is where the ideas come from in business. You will always need new and fresh ideas. Listen to the people around you and the people you socialize with. Remember, sometimes you may get your inspiration from others. Think about those individuals and why they inspire you.

Commitment means that you are as good as your word. What you say you are going to do, you will do. You set a good example and people respond to it.

Belief means that you first believe in yourself, and then others will follow. If you don't believe in the course that you've chosen, the people around you cannot possibly follow you. Be sure you are confident and consistent in your beliefs.

Self-control means that you remain calm and even tempered. Do not let others control your emotions. People (patients or staff) will push your buttons. Try to remain calm, cool, and collected. Save comments for a professional conversation when appropriate. In many cases this conversation will occur after business hours.

Endeavor is perseverance. A successful business takes enormous, tireless effort.

Faith involves first having confidence in yourself and also having confidence in the people around you, as well as the work they are trying to do for you and your company. No matter how much drive and determination you have, you cannot achieve success by yourself. The people around you will ultimately allow you to grow and create a successful business.

Willpower or unwavering strength is absolutely necessary to succeed in business. Things will not always go as planned, so be prepared. After decades of experience in owning a small business, I can tell you that, of all the personal characteristics of leadership, you will depend on your willpower to get up day after day, to continue to be creative and prosperous, and to build your team and your business.

Patience is essential because success happens over time, not overnight. The quicker you rise, the quicker you can sink. Consistency over time will bring positive results whether that is in your personal life, your business life, or your financial life. Do not rush it; take your time, and good things will happen.

We just devoted a considerable amount of time reviewing basic principles and leadership qualities needed to be truly successful in your business and personal life. Your business must follow certain leadership steps. It is critical that you have the tools and information to build the infrastructure, and that you surround yourself with quality people to bring your practice to a success. In business, we call this series of steps an Administration Scale. This scale is comprised of several components including: purpose, programs, policies, projects, goals, plans, orders, ideal scenes, nonexistence, statistics, conditions of exchange, danger, valuable final products, scale of conditions, emergencies, normal conditions, power change, production of affluence, conditional formulas, change of your operation basis, power conditions, promotion, economizing actions, delivery, and stiffened discipline.

The next thing that is critical is to understand what each of these steps in the scale can do for you and your business.

Purpose refers to educating and motivating patients about the importance of dental health and overall health. There are several ways to improve a patient's dental health. They include providing treatment plans, informing your patients of helpful products on the market, and reducing a patient's overall dental cost associated with poor dental care.

Programs are a series of steps, taken in the correct sequence, that are necessary to carry out a plan. You must renew and review new and existing dental products and services. Review both internal and external marketing policies. Implement monthly meetings by e-mail or by impromptu face-to-face meetings. Review and revise all steps associated with your business, from the initial patient contact on the phone or at the front desk, throughout the entire course of care and service, to the delivery of your final product. The follow-up of that final product and service can be even more important in enabling you to determine your company's strengths, weaknesses, opportunities, and threats.

Policies are a set of rules or guidelines by which a group conducts its affairs in order to achieve its goals and purposes. You must hire the right personnel and then train and educate those people so they have the right tools and know how to use them effectively. You must provide clear and effective treatment plans that have value and that are attainable by your patients. Remember, even though your patients may be unable to afford the treatment at this time, they deserve to know the options and what you feel is the best course of treatment. Remember that you have to understand the relationship between time and money; spending two hours on a treatment plan that is unattainable makes little sense. Consider written treatment plans that provide options in a much more efficient manner.

Projects are a written sequence of steps needed to complete a task. Projects should have a time frame in which to increase quality, decrease time, and improve results. They should be evaluated and reviewed daily and monthly to ensure you are getting the results you expect. The project should improve efficiency in all aspects. Improvement project creation involves asking "What is the plan?" and "How was it coordinated?" Many times, we will start projects, but we will not complete them. Be sure that your projects are completed, and that people are held accountable for completing those projects.

Goals are really an objective; they are the design of your future and overall guide. Your dental organization should have a goal. An example of a great goal for any organization is to be the best, most profitable, and enjoyable dental facility anywhere. Keep in mind that everyone's goal can be different--the most important point is to *have* a goal.

Plans are the outlines of the general action steps that are to be taken by the owner and employees. You must utilize the computer hardware and software that are available to help execute your plan. In every office, there will be systems (for example, meetings, interoffice communication, office manuals, intranet) in place to make your plan available to all employees. Make sure they know the reasons for these plans. This action plan is extremely important to communicate effectively and to motivate yourself, the people around you, and your patient base.

Orders and assignments are specific actions by which you get things done. They are usually done in a short period of time and involve who does what, when, why, and where. Be certain that your orders and assignments accomplish tasks and that they follow an overall stratgetic plan.

Ideal scenes are a vision of the way a business ideally should be run, and the vision is 100 percent in agreement with the goals of that business. You must allow your patients to find value in their care, and they must become emotional advocates of the practice. This will create a situation where they don't miss appointments, they pay their bills, and they refer other patients to you. When this plan is followed correctly, your patients receive something more important than dental restorations—they receive value. Value is something that has worth to someone else; there is generally an exchange process of offering something valuable in return for some other valuable service or object. In addition, the value of sales and delivery is extremely important, and you must always deliver on what you've promised to your patients and employees.

Nonexistence is a term used when nothing is produced and there is no valuable final product. If the group, organization, or business does not provide a valuable final product, it is all over.

Statistics are used to track information and data to determine whether your business is following the correct path. Although there are no limits to the number of statistics and reports that can be generated with today's software, the following is a good guideline in tracking the health of your organization:

Are your patients making appointments?

Are they accepting your treatment plan?

Are they referring other family members and patients to you?

Are they paying on the way out for their care and service?

What is the revenue produced on a day-to-day basis?

Determine how many new patients you are receiving on a month-to-month basis and the sources of those new patients. You should also be tracking how many patients are leaving your practice and for what reasons. Here are examples of questions to ask:

Are your fees too high?

Are your patients dissatisfied?

Are you not accepting their insurance plans?

Are your hours inconvenient?

Check your accounts receivables. What percentage of the dollars each month is associated with your insurance companies not paying because of inaccuracies in your billing systems or mistakes by the insurance companies? This problem would be tracked under unsubmitted or incomplete dental insurance claims.

Another useful statistic would be to track the number of patients and the amount of money in accounts receivables of those patients who have not made any payment at all for sixty days or longer. This certainly is a red flag that there is a problem with the insurance, a problem with the care or service, or a combination of both.

Conditions of an exchange cover four areas: a criminal exchange, a partial exchange, a fair exchange, and an exchange in abundance. In a criminal exchange, you provide no value and you have cheated your patient or employee (such as doing a crown when a filling would be fine). In a partial exchange, you and your patient or employee get some benefit (such as selling a product that has a benefit, but may not actually be needed). A fair exchange occurs when a patient receives the treatment that is needed and promised. An exchange in abundance is very rare, however, is the key to success and expansion, not just in business but also in life. In simple terms, you are delivering more value than what the people around you expect.

Danger simply means, in business, the end is near, and immediate action is necessary. Business decisions must be handled immediately; there can be no more delays. The statistics are showing a continuing steady decline, plunging downward in every category, and rapidly exploding. Senior executives are finding themselves doing the jobs of others. Your business is in trouble, danger is near, and immediate action must be taken. It is critical that you, as a leader and an owner, understand and know when danger is around the corner.

Valuable final product (VFP) means either goods or services as a completed product. VFP is the total package or end result. This means total care from the initial patient phone call to the final follow-up phone call to check on your patient who is happy and pleased with your care and service. Patient satisfaction is based on the high quality of the valuable final product, which means in all cases your patients have found value in your care and service. Keep in mind that the final product has a series of sub products that can make or break your end results. If all goes well, your patients and staff become raving fans!

Scales of condition are a series of business issues that ultimately lead to an end product, which in our case, is dental care and service. The following list (going from high to low) is a series of conditions to help guide you and your business to success. They are power, power change, affluence, normal, emergency, danger, and nonexistence. Strive to keep your business operating in the upper four categories which are power, change, affluence, and normal.

Emergencies are critical situations that occur when the production and the collection are not what they should be. The statistics are unchanging, the trends are in a downward direction, and if no action is taken, things will fall apart. Remember, things never stay the same—they are either expanding or contracting.

Normal conditions are simply when things are running neither extraordinarily well nor poorly—they are just fairly steady.

Power change happens under only two conditions: when you are so successful it is time to turn your business over to someone else, or when you are very unsuccessful, and it is time to turn your business over to someone else. The old business motto is, "Sell on the upside, buy on the downside." For decades I have evaluated dental practices all over Western Massachusetts, and I have consistently found that people are always trying to sell on the downside. That means the value of their organizations are significantly less, and their return on investment is significantly less. Please think about that power exchange. If you are considering purchasing, look for the bargain, providing you can make the changes to improve the business. If you are considering selling, attempt to get your business in order and on track, and you will get a much better price.

Affluence is a steep increase in statistics such as an increase in the number of new patients, an increase in revenue, or both. This is a state in which your business will be strong and healthy, and you will feel good about yourself and your organization.

Conditional formulas include an emergency plan. This plan begins with promoting something within the care and service of your business, such as decreasing patient waiting time, improving scheduling, and improving delivery of care. By implementing this plan, your business becomes more organized and efficient in all aspects of operations.

Operational basis change occurs when you can no longer go about business as usual because that is what caused the problem in the first place. Do not be afraid of change. It can be extremely beneficial, if it is done correctly. Over decades of running a small business, a consistent mistake I have seen is owners hesitating to make changes. Remember, there is a difference between a good change and a bad change; the key is to think it through before taking the action steps, not after. Recognize what operational changes are needed, and those changes must be implemented and evaluated.

Power conditions are an even better situation than affluence. In these conditions, the statistics have gone to an extremely high range, your business, services, and care are performing at a higher level than you even anticipated, and there is such an abundance of production that the momentary halts or dips do not even appear to occur. It almost appears that your business cannot fail. It is usually temporary, so enjoy this time of abundance!

Promotion is the ability to market yourself, your business, and employees along with the services. Advertise, knock on doors, call existing patients, and talk up your organization and its people. Get involved to make it better. If you are not promoting yourself and your organization, no one else is. In cases of "emergency," or you are in "danger," most organizations will cut advertising, but in almost all cases, this is the wrong approach.

Economizing actions are the steps you have taken to put your organization in the correct direction. These newly implemented steps such as marketing, review of processes and procedures, (which have improved care and service), and revised budget need to continue, even when the statistics start improving. Do not go back to the old way of doing things. Hold on to profits in order to continue to build a valuable final product and service.

Deliverly means being prepared to do whatever needs to be done in order to produce a desired outcome. In order to deliver more goods and services, be sure you have all the right tools and people in place. Be prepared, ready, and willing to deliver your final valuable product and service.

Stiffened discipline involves getting better at all aspects of your job. For some, it means becoming better and faster at delivering treatment and services. For others, it means better communication between staff and patients. Learn how to sell, lead, and organize. You and your organization will ultimately suffer without discipline.

I hope that, at this point, you have established a good understanding of some building blocks that are basic to all successful business relationships. Next, it is important for you to evaluate good profits and bad profits. Some people are not aware of it, but there is such a thing as bad profits. These are profits that are earned at the expense of customer relationships, as when a customer feels misled, mistreated, or ignored. Bad profits happen when a company saves money by delivering an undesirable patient/customer experience. They extract the value from patients/customers instead of adding value.

What leads to bad profits? Failure to recognize weaknesses in yourself and your company due to lack of training. In addition, bad profits are a result of leadership failing to understand themselves and their organization and how that organization works. What I mean by this is you have to understand your team and what motivates and moves them. If such messages are not clear and consistent, you do not know what the goals of the organization really are. In addition, a lack of clarity about the goals, how to achieve these goals, or why you should want to achieve these goals will all lead to bad profits. In most cases, the success of an organization is determined by the amount of money or profit it makes.

You should recognize that bad profits create what are called business detractors. These are people who hurt us and our organization. They drive up our costs, and they create the majority of our problems, and they waste you and your company's time and effort. They will badmouth your company's reputation and put a stranglehold on growth because they have had a bad experience with your company. They can demoralize the organization and the people in it. If profits are bad profits, you will be a short-term success, but in the long-term, a failure. Remember this lesson because all practitioners can slip into this category; and many times without even realizing it.

Establish a culture among yourself, your family, and your organization that you and your staff will be proud of. It should be a culture that deals with problems rather than avoids them. Be sure that you are doing the job, providing care and service, and that you actually understand the essence of your job and what it creates for your organization. The owner(s) should be able to provide a message to his/her organization, managers, and team along with patients that is clear and concise. The manager(s) should be able to take that message and bring it back to their team. The managers should make sure that the numbers and the results of your organization statistics are effective and reproducable. It is important, if not mandatory, that oversight of these managers is followed, to ensure the data obtained from these statistics is accurate and putting your organization on the good profit track.

In the end, what is most important to achieving and maintaining success is establishing relationships with your staff and your patients. These bonds are cultivated with time, patience, and understanding. This effort must come not only from you, but also from everyone in your organization. Still, it starts with the front line, the people who answer the phone and create your image and your culture. Keep in mind that, in most cases, the effort to build relationships also ends with that front line, since the last thing your patients will deal with is the person checking out your patients. In many cases, the front desk coordinator job is left to someone who is inexperienced. The person who sees your patients both first and last should be experienced clinically, as well as in sales and marketing. Please remember that the first and last contact that patients have may leave a lasting impression.

The opposite of detractors are promoters. These are people who market the practice, and they are the loyal patients who see us over and over again. Time after time, they believe us, they like us, and they trust our organization. Promoters provide the most cost-effective growth. More importantly, they are loyal. Keep in mind that the value of promoters in your practice cannot be overstated.

How can we avoid detractors and attract promoters? First, to avoid detractors, you must excel in service. Along with this, communicate clearly and concisely to your staff and patients. Provide an ideal patient environment, written treatment plans, and clear financial arrangements. Prepare the patient before a treatment and follow up afterward. Dentists and patients must understand clearly the risks, the benefits, and alternatives to the care they are seeking. In order to achieve attracting promoters you must allow the appropriate time to deliver this exceptional care and service. You *must* be able to identify detractors.

You will recognize these detractors with experience. They are not happy with anyone or anything. Every doctor is bad, and it is always someone else's fault. The negative effects of detractors cannot be overstated. Beware of these individuals, they will ruin your life and hurt your business.

It is important to be able to measure promoters and detractors. This awareness is accomplished by the use of a net promoter score, sometimes referred to as an NPS. It simply means that there are three types of patients: promoters, detractors, and passive patients. The passive patients are satisfied, but they are not enthusiastic patients. These patients can be easily attracted to another office or competitor. The goal in a practice is to have 100 percent promoters. The best companies in the world seem to have a net promoter score of between 42 and 82 percent. Increasing your net promoter score improves the bottom line for your organization or business, but it will also significantly improve the quality of your life.

In order to determine this net promoter score, the measurements are made by looking at your most satisfied patients; those patients who desire to make referrals to your organization and return to your office for future care and treatment. Understanding the value of a high net promoter score will allow you to improve the retention rate of your patients, increase your margins, and allow you to increase your annual spending. This knowledge will provide improved cost efficiencies, as well as significantly improve your word of mouth, advertising, and increase your market share. Keep in mind that the value of promoters in your practice cannot be overstated. The goal in any business is to remove the detractors, continue to cultivate the promoters, and move the passive patients into the promoter category. This goal will not only lead to a successful business practice, but will also significantly improve the quality of your life.

The next area that needs to be explored is looking deeper at the patients you will be treating day to day. Keep in mind that the following discussion can also be associated with your infrastructure or staff members. The DISC personality evaluation is as follows. Most people will fall into one of these four categories, and in many cases, the individual will be a combination of these personalities. However, in the combination there will be one dominant type of personality.

The *D* stands for dominant, direct, decisive, and determined; someone who is a doer.

The *I* stands for inspirational, influential, interactive, and impressive; that is, someone who is interested in people and is outgoing, task oriented, and people oriented.

The *S* stands for steady, stable, supportive, and sensitive; someone who is a specialist.

The *C* stands for cautious, calculating, competent, compliant, and careful (as in reserved and understanding).

The ability to recognize and understand these types of personalities will not only help you relate better to your staff, but also with your patients. As you are discussing financial arrangements and treatment plans with patients, please consider the *D*, the *I*, the *S*, and the *C* types.

The Myers-Briggs analysis test evaluates whether a person is stimulated by the extroverted or introverted people around them. It helps calculate how people make decisions. Are they the thinking type of people, or the feeling type of people? Of concern is whether a person gathers information by studying it or by intuition. It is how a person experiences life, either judging or perceiving. The combination of understanding the Myers-Briggs analysis and the DISC personality evaluation will significantly help you coordinate, motivate, and influence your staff and your patients. Do not miscalculate the power of emotions; it is what moves and motivates people and business.

There is another acronym, DDD, which can be defined as a process to design a winning customer strategy.

- The first *D* stands for design—you design the appropriate segmentation for your patient base and create a complete patient experience in each of the segments.
- The next *D* stands for delivery—every department and employee must pull in the same direction.
- The third *D* stands for develop—reinvent and renew your patient experience over and over again; you must change for the better.

Keep in mind that in many cases you will be acting as a manager, or you will be hiring people to manage. Understand that most managers feel accountable only for improving profits. Most do not feel accountable for improving patient relationships or the quality of those relationships. Successful managers, just like successful leaders, must possess a combination of both.

As you embark on your new position, you must understand and implement the necessary steps for the creation of a *SPECIAL* practice.

The *S* in *SPECIAL* stands for scheduling. The schedule must be efficient and effectively planned each and every day.

The *P* in *SPECIAL* stands for production, understanding which procedures are the most productive and which procedures are the least productive. In all businesses, you must understand that you will not always be productive. It is part of business. (Remember, service always trumps production.)

The *E* in *SPECIAL* stands for your employees. If your employees are not trained and retrained, motivated, and engaged, then you will never have a *special* practice.

The *C* stands for collections. In any business, the goal is to collect 100 percent of what is produced. In reality, this is almost always impossible. In the field of dentistry, however, the goal is certainly to stay above 97 percent.

The *I* stands for internal controls--the processes by which your assets are protected, liabilities are reduced, and data from reports are maintained and evaluated. Every section of your business must have internal controls.

The *A* stands for the associates-- how you find them, how you keep them, and how you train and motivate them.

The *L* stands for liabilities--the assessment of your liabilities determines how to minimize your expenses, how to know when to purchase assets, and how to know when to hold off.

Using *SPECIAL* as an acronym will help to keep you focused on the areas of your business that must be well organized, maintained, and evaluated. If you accomplish those tasks, you truly will have a special practice.

In regard to scheduling, nothing will affect your business and your quality of life more than a successful and well thought-out schedule. The schedule is the barometer of your practice; it creates almost all the stress and problems in your business. If you do not understand and control it, your life and business will be out of balance. For most patients, early mornings from seven o'clock until nine o'clock would be considered prime time. Around lunch time, between 11:00 a.m. and 2:00 p.m., would also be considered prime time. The evenings and Saturdays and holidays would certainly be considered prime time. As you evaluate your schedule, those particular areas should be selected for the promoters in your practice, the individuals who are busy and help build your practice.

Dead time, those difficult times to schedule, are generally from nine o'clock in the morning until eleven o'clock and from two o'clock in the afternoon until four o'clock. I strongly recommend that you reserve these more difficult times for elderly or retired patients when scheduling by production.

High production is highly profitable items that generate the greatest return on your investment. Those highly profitable appointments should be delegated to Saturdays and evenings. Most people would prefer not to work evenings or Saturdays, so if that dentist is going to sacrifice his or her personal time for the good of the business, it should be the most profitable time to schedule. When dealing with production you must understand that high ticket items that take a long time are sometimes much less productive than lower ticket items that can be completed in a much shorter period of time. For example, in many cases the sealant can be placed on a tooth in a relatively short period of time, much like a fluoridation treatment. Both of these treatments on the surface would appear as low production because the overall cost seems small. In reality, however, these procedures can be delegated to staff members and can be done in an extremely short period of time. Thus, they can actually be more profitable than higher ticket items such as crowns, bridges, and implant surgery. These more complicated procedures take a greater length of time to complete the treatment, and may also create many more post-operative problems, and generally have a much higher overhead associated with their production.

As with patients, when dealing with employees, I would strongly recommend that you consider the profile of the employees. Look at the person's age, past work history, ability, and the probability of that employee staying invested in your business for a long period of time. As a general rule, I believe males and females over the age of thirty-five whose children no longer need to be monitored on a 24-7 basis are many times some of your best employees. I personally feel that, out of all the traits I have studied in decades of hiring employees, dedication, determination, and stick-to-itiveness are the qualities that I look for. If I had to name one quality that trumps all other qualities, though, it would be loyalty. In any business there are ups and downs, peaks and valleys. The loyal employee will stick by you through thick and thin. Hiring an associate is a two-way street, and in many cases, particularly in dentistry, the owner of the practice is extremely inexperienced in knowing what to look for in an excellent associate, and the associate is inexperienced and does not know what to look for in a practice.

I have addressed these areas in earlier chapters, and I strongly recommend that both parties give a considerable amount of time to the following. Consider whether or not there is an adequate patient base. Also consider whether or not there is an adequate infrastructure, as well as scheduled time to mentor and monitor your associate. I would also recommend that before you consider hiring an associate, be certain they are willing to commit for a minimum of two years. The time, the energy, and the money spent to prepare an associate properly, only to see him/her leave for one reason or another in less than two years, is truly not a profitable route to take for either party.

Remember that collection can be a double-edged sword. If your collection policies are too strict, you will find that your production numbers will be relatively low. If your collection procedures are too relaxed, you will create accounts receivables that will be very high. As a general rule, I strongly recommend that your accounts receivables do not exceed forty-five days of production. Generally, what I mean by this is, if an office produces $100,000 in a thirty-day period, forty-five days of production would mean $150,000. If the accounts receivables are in excess of $150, 000, then generally you may have internal control issues, insurance problems, and collection problems, and a red flag should arise. If the collection is less than $150,000, you may be losing or missing opportunities because your collection procedures and policies are so strict that patients are refusing treatment to avoid difficulties in payment.

You must be able to review your standard reports on a daily or weekly basis and have checks and balances for every area of your practice. In my opinion, you should be 100 percent responsible for all checks going out of your office and be able to reconcile all dollars coming into your practice. After evaluating associates for decades, I find that the associates lacked experience, not just in clinical skills, but in communication skills. I would strongly recommend that if you do not have adequate time to mentor, teach, observe, and monitor, you are probably not ready for an associate.

The liabilities in any business can be enormous. Be sure that your practice becomes a corporation, whether it is a limited liability company or a limited liability partnership. I am sure your accountant and legal team can help direct you, but I would strongly suggest that you create and get involved with the corporate structure that protects your assets, reduces your liability, improves your tax situation, and allows you to expand easily or divest.

We now get down to the "brass tacks" of discussing treatment planning. If all your other areas of business are in order, the treatment plan is perhaps the most important aspect of creating a successful business. A good treatment plan must start with two major areas.

One area is to create and maintain complete, comprehensive, and clear patient records. In the field of dentistry, charting should evaluate:

- existing restorations and potentially new restorations
- intra- and extraoral diagnostic photographs
- diagnostic radiographs that include horizontal and vertical bite wings
- a panoramic survey
- when indicated, a full-mouth series of radiographs along with upper and lower diagnostic impressions or digital impressions along with mounted models

For the evaluation of soft tissue, it is imperative to include:

- pocket depths
- bleeding upon probing
- mobility and furcation
- occlusal wear patterns
- recession and lack of attached gingiva

The overall assessment of the dental hygiene, along with an extensive medical and dental history must be done. After decades of treatment, the red flags that appear to me when evaluating the patient include

- a very poor dental IQ on the patient's part
- a smoker who smokes more than a pack of cigarettes a day

- someone who drinks more than two ounces of alcohol a day
- an uncontrolled diabetic

It is my experience that a patient who has superb hygiene and performs meticulous home care will keep all dental treatment in good shape for a long period of time. However, the most exquisite dentistry in a patient who does not have excellent home care will, in almost all cases, fail rapidly.

Another area that might be overlooked in a dental practice is open contacts or poor contacts in existing restorations. Once this information has been collected, it is imperative that the dentist is able to assimilate it into a comprehensive treatment plan that makes sense for the patient, not only clinically, but also financially. Once the clinical records have been provided, the next part is to be able to have a financial policy in place and the ability of you and your staff to communicate clearly and concisely the value to the patient. If the patient cannot evaluate the *value* of care, he/she will not proceed with your recommended treatment, no matter how correct the treatment plan is.

The second part of the communication equation is critical. It is extremely important to communicate clearly, to motivate your patient to proceed with the treatment plan that has been recommended, and to show value to your recommended treatment plan. I am acutely aware that some individuals clearly have a much better gift at communication, sales, and marketing than others. For those individuals who are very weak in these areas and are unable to improve in these areas, I strongly recommend that you look for someone within your dental team to provide the strengths in these areas where you have weaknesses. Whether you call this individual a treatment plan coordinator, a marketing person, or a front desk coordinator, it does not matter. If that individual is vested in your practice and has the skills that you lack, utilize them for the good of your business and the financial success of your business.

In the end, you the dentist or trained team member must be able to evaluate all areas of the clinical practice of dentistry. This will include a working knowledge of removable and fixed prostheses, periodontics, orthodontics, oral surgical procedures, implants, and temporomandibular joint issues. In addition, your office must be able to educate your patients about their dental health through communication, motivation, along with providing financial planning options and scheduling the patient. This information should be written and provided to the patient with a list of associated fees so that the patient can make an informed decision.

Developing a comprehensive treatment plan can be time consuming. I recommend that every patient have a comprehensive treatment plan. Before investing enormous amounts of time and money, you should have an understanding of that patient's financial interests and abilities. Clearly, an unemployed person with significant financial restrictions may not be able to accept a comprehensive plan. Keep in mind that you should still offer and explain the treatment plan, but the speed and time you spend on this treatment plan must be guarded. This simply means the patient may not be in a position at that moment to go forward with the treatment, but down the road, the patient certainly may be able to afford your treatment plan and will appreciate the time and energy you spent for their best dental care and health. In the end, your patient will go forward only if motivated. As discussed earlier in this book, the motivating factors for most patients are the following:

- The fear that delaying treatment could eventually cause more painful and more time-consuming dental treatment
- The financial concern that delayed treatment may cost significantly more time and money down the road
- The desire to feel better about themselves through a better smile, a better color and shape to their teeth, or better comfort; that is, ultimately, they want to look and feel better
- The value they see in the time and money they invest in their care

In order for these four entities to work properly, that patient must believe you, like you, and trust you. If that triangle is not complete, in the long term the patient will ask for his or her money back or the patient will fall into the detractor category.

When discussing treatment with your patients, I cannot emphasize enough that you keep it simple: "Mr. Smith, your tooth is broken." "Ms. Smith, you have an infection." "Mr. Smith, you have a broken tooth and an infection." For decades, I have been providing care in a large practice, seeing over 900 new patients in one month. All of these patients have come from other dental offices. After evaluating associates and their communication skills, I have seen consistently their ability to destroy the reputation of dentistry and the reputation of their peers. There is not a practicing physician or dentist who has not made iatrogenic errors. In some cases the errors are patient-induced. In some cases the errors are a combination of both doctor and patient.

If you tell Ms. Smith that she has calculus underneath the gums, she could say to you that she just had her teeth cleaned last month. If you tell Mr. Smith he has margins open on his crowns, bridges, and restorations, he may say they were just done a little while ago. If you tell Ms. Smith that the reason the root canal is failing is that the dentist came up short in his or her fill, she might state that she had the root canal done within the last six months. If you tell Mr. Smith that his teeth are crowded and out of position, he may tell you he just finished two years of orthodontics. What kind of message are you sending to each and every one of these patients? You could be implying it is the dentist's fault, but it also could be the patient's fault. Think for a moment-- did the patient refused to wear a retainer? Did the patient ask that the orthodontics be completed sooner rather than later? Did you consider that the patient has a maximum opening of only 20 or 25 mm and he or she is a gagger, so it is difficult, if not impossible, to get an accurate impression, whether it is digital or otherwise?

Remember you should be motivated to do only the best care for your patients. However, because of time constraints, and financial restraints, or insurance restraints, less than ideal care occurs. My personal opinion is that you need to try to avoid all of these pitfalls that not only do harm to our profession, but also accomplish nothing for our patients. The patient has a problem, and you should have a solution to that problem. The goal is to provide the best dentistry you can under the conditions that you are presented with. Anyone who has practiced dentistry for any period of time understands that, in many cases, compromise is necessary. Almost every patient who will walk into your dental practice is coming in because of a problem. My recommendation again is to keep it simple. Inform Mr. or Ms. Smith that the *tooth* is broken, that he/she has an infection, or the *tooth* is broken and there is an infection. Over and over again, I hear the associates say, "The *filling* is broken," or "The *crown* is broken." The average patient will immediately think, that the previous dentist did something wrong. Remember to consider that perhaps the patient, instead of doing the crown to begin with, may have requested the dentist to do less than ideal care. When another dental professional judges another practioner's treatment and skill, it is a disservice to our profession. That old adage "If you cannot say something nice, do not say anything at all" could not be more true. Since I am not in the dental chair, and I am not privy to hearing or see how the treatment was performed and why the treatment was performed, I strongly recommend that you never judge your peers. Judge only yourself; you should strive to be proud of the care and treatment you provide and keep your peers out of the equation.

New associates will make the following ten mistakes. The objective here is to have you recognize these mistakes and avoid or minimize them. These tips will help you create your special practice and make your career in dentistry much more successful.

Mistake number one: You will start out at a job that you should not have accepted. Please take the time to make sure that the job you accept is the job that you hope you can stay with for the rest of your life. The time, money, aggravation, and stress of having to change locations and organizations is enormous to you.

Mistake number two: You take too long to leave that job. When you are dissatisfied, I strongly recommend, as soon as problems occur, that you set up a meeting and immediately try to resolve them. In most cases, the associate feels trapped and will stay in that position too long, wasting vital resources, time, and money.

Mistake number three: You become too friendly with your patients and staff. You are now a professional business man or woman. Keep your relationships on a business level. When you get too involved with your patients or staff, problems will occur, and eventually all parties will be unhappy. As I say to my children, there are times when I am your friend, but there are times when I have to act as a parent. If you get too friendly with your staff and your patients, there comes a point when you will have to act as a boss, employer, or clinician, and it will cause problems.

Mistake number four: You have poor business knowledge or no business knowledge. Today with the internet, data and knowledge surround you. You should be familiar with basic business concepts as well as basic marketing and sales. The majority of people whom I deal with have absolutely no business guidance or experience at all. It is not necessary for you to get a master's in business, but basic business knowledge is paramount. Focus on fundamental accounting principles such as understanding a balance sheet, income statements, and a statement of cash flow. You should understand the SWOT analysis: strength, weaknesses, opportunities, and threats. Understand basic sales and communication skills to improve your practice.

Mistake number five: In most cases, you are unclear about when and how to refer patients out of your practice. I recommend that when you get involved in your new career, you surround yourself with specialists that you believe, like, and trust. Remember that, as a general dentist, you are the quarterback of the team. It is your responsibility to follow the care and treatment and make sure that your patients end up back in your practice for follow-up care. A good referral source is not a best friend. It is someone who has a philosophy about clinical care that matches your own and will have your patient's best interests at heart as well as your business. Make sure that your patient base stays in your practice.

Mistake number six: You are unfamiliar and uncomfortable with marketing yourself. There should be an announcement on radio, TV, newspaper, and internet when you start your new position. There should be advertisements in the office complete with a printed CV of your background and your history. This information should go to all the surrounding towns so that the patient base is aware of your presence. Have your own set of business cards and make sure the office website has your CV along with your photo. Be sure to personally meet all employees involved in your office. I recommend that you have an e-mail that is available to all of your staff members.

Mistake number seven: You communicate poorly with your patients. We have touched on it extensively, but to summarize and review, remember the following. Rather than question previous care, you simply say, "You have an infection, but we can solve your problem." "You have a broken tooth, but we can solve your problem." "You have an infection and a broken tooth, but we can solve your problem."

Mistake number eight: Signing an employment agreement, if you do not understand it. There are times when you just need to spend the money and effort for experts. Have the employment agreement reviewed by a professional so that you have proper protection and you understand the agreement that you will sign.

Mistake number nine: The type of practice you are joining is not what you expected. You are dissatisfied because you did not do your due diligence, you are confused, you realize the complexion of the practice is not what you expected. Your patient base may be mostly insurance, private, or a mixture of both. You were not aware of what that patient base was made of, but now you are involved with DMOs and PPOs. You were not clear on the financial office policies, you were not clear on your benefits, you were not clear on your compensation package, and you were not clear on the types of treatment you would be performing. Over decades of care, I have heard the same thing from associate after associate. "All I do all day long is prophys. So why can't I do other types of treatment?" "Why don't I have my own dental assistant?" "Why don't I have the supplies and the equipment that I need to perform the care I thought I would be doing?" Be sure to devote the time and effort necessary into your due diligence by reviewing your employment contract.

Mistake number ten: You leave the organization or practice on bad terms. Try to leave on good terms. Find a time when you and your employer both have the time to speak. Write down what you like and what you do not like. Be sure you have an exit interview. Leave a forwarding e-mail or address in case you need to be contacted. Leaving on bad terms accomplishes nothing. We live in a very small world and, trust me, over time your paths will cross again. In addition, both parties will benefit from this learning experience.

I would like to provide some information about a new or existing business structure for those of you considering opening up your dental practice from scratch, or if you are considering taking over an existing dental practice. This is important for the seasoned dentist and the new associate. In general, a business entity is created to provide a service, a product, or both. The structure of the business entity is to control your business risks and your taxes. When we talk about risks, there are personal liabilities, which are liabilities created by an individual. An example would be a car accident in which the at-fault driver is personally liable for the injuries and property damage caused by the accident. There are also business liabilities. These are liabilities created by the business entity itself. An example would be a commercial loan. In this example, a business borrows money to purchase equipment. However, if you personally guarantee that loan, the obligation converges to both the business and your personal liability.

The next type of liability is considered professional liability. Dentists, physicians, CPAs, and attorneys are all subjected to liabilities for the services they render in a professional capacity. This means a business entity cannot protect professionals from malpractice negligence or other professional liabilities.

What are some different business entities that you should be aware of? There are corporations, partnerships or sole proprietorships. Each of these entities have 5 basic parts. They are formation, liability of the owner or owners, management, transferability and taxation. A brief summary may be helpful. There are two types of corporations: C-Corporations and S-Corporations. A C-Corporation is a taxable entity. In a professional C corporation, any profits that remain in the corporation at the end of the year are taxed at 35% at the entity level. Profits removed from a C- Corporation, outside of payroll, are considered a dividend. This dividend, or removal of profits, is not a reduction of profits, and is taxed at the corporate level as part of the total income and at the individual level as a dividend income. This is where the term "double-taxation" comes from. All income is reported in a federal form 1120. All corporations begin as a C-Corporation, but can be converted to an S-Corporation by filing and IRS form 2553. S-Corporations are designed to be flow-through entity and therefore not subject to "double-taxation" as noted above. There is no entity level tax in an S-Corporation. The profits of the practice flow directly to the individual shareholders and are taxed on the individual tax return only. Any withdrawals of profits from an S-Corporation are considered a "shareholder distribution of profits" and avoid payroll taxes, but not income taxes. The primary benefits of an S-Corporation are the avoidance of payroll taxes and "double-taxation" on the distribution of profits. Most corporations in the dental industry are structured as S- Corporations. All income is reported on a federal form 1120S.

Partnerships are another entity structure. There are 3 types of partnerships: Gerneral Partnerships (GP), Limited Liability Partnerships (LLP), and Limited Liability Companies (LLC). These three entities are set up as partnerships for tax purposes. The only difference between a GP and a LLP or LLC is liability protection. An LLC and LLP limit the liability of the individual partners from both the other partners and outside risks. A partnership is extremely flexible in regard to the allocation of income. The partners can choose to allocate income any way they want and not necessarily by ownership. A partnership is also a flow-through entity, similar to an S-corporation, for tax purposes and therefore is not subject to an corporate tax. All of the income, however, is subject to self-employment (payroll) taxes and is taxed on the individual tax return. All income is reported on a federal form 1065. The third entity type is a sole proprietor. This is simply the same as an independent contractor. The income is reported on the Schedule C on a personal income tax return and is subject to self-employment (payroll) taxes, along with income taxes. This structure offers no liability protection from your personal assets. Limited Liability Companies (LLC), have become very popular in the last several years, and can be structured for tax purposes as any of the entities noted above; C-Corporation, S-Corporation, partnership or sole proprietor. It helps to provide additional liability protection for a partnership and sole proprietor while keeping the tax structure the same. Professional corporations prior to 1986 were very popular since they offered favorable tax treatment, which allowed owners of the PC to shelter more money from taxation than a sole proprietor or partnership could. However, since 1986, corporations are taxed at a flat rate.

If your primary income is generated from the business, I suggest you focus on the tax considerations as the most important factor, and liability issues as secondary consideration. On the other hand, if the entity that you will be putting your personal assets into generates no income or little income, I would recommend a focus on the limitations of liability as the primary factor for you and your entity.

At some point, it will be necessary for you to review a practice evaluation, whether it be your own practice to sell, or a practice you are considering investing in. Some basic terms and information may be helpful. There is investment value, fair market value, going concern value, degree of marketability, and book value. I will start with investment value. This is the value to a particular investor based on individual investment requirements. It is different from fair market value, which is impersonal and unattached and does not include investment value. However, investment value does include fair market value. In most cases, this is not a system used in valuing a professional practice. Book value is really a misnomer because it does not represent a value at all; rather, it is an accounting term, not an evaluation term. It means the sum of the assets accounts netted of depreciation and amortization less the liability accounts as shown on a balance sheet. The longer the assets or the liability is on the books, the less identifiable the relationships going concern.

Value is an assumption about the status of the business. It assumes the business is being valued as a viable operating entity. It has assets and inventory in place, along with the workforce, and its doors are open for business. Fair market value is many times the most accepted standard. It is the amount at which property would change hands between a willing seller and a willing buyer. Both the willing seller and buyer, of course, are hypothetical. It assumes prevalent market conditions at the date of the valuation. The degree of marketability is the ability to sell or liquidate. The benchmark is an actively traded stock. The quicker an entity can be sold, the less risk and the higher the value.

The valuation methods fall into three broad categories: the cost value approach, the market value approach, and the income value approach. There are additional methods, such as discounted cash flow, capitalization of earnings, multiple of revenues, excess earnings, asset accumulation and depreciation, goodwill, and comparative transaction. There are also punitive and retirement formulas.

As in most issues, there are advantages and disadvantages to each evaluation method. My personal opinion is that you should consider the following. Take the last three years of the net collected money in the practice and take a percentage of between 32 and 62 percent to calculate the value. Therefore, if the business has net collected on average $1 million in each of the last three years, the value that you would pay for that practice would be between $320,000 and $620,000. This method is simple, and it is easy to remember. You may ask why there is such a large fluctuation. There are many factors that will need to be addressed along with the simple equation. One of the factors is whether the existing owner is willing to stay on. If he/she is unwilling to remain as an employee and help the transfer of patients and staff, then obviously the lower percentage would apply.

The next issue to be evaluated is the condition of the facility and the capital improvements that will be necessary to bring the office up to the point that you would consider it viable and acceptable. I also think another important component is the amount of free cash that can be determined from the individual owner's tax returns. Clearly, if there is not enough free cash to pay for the finance of debt on the purchase of the practice, then quite honestly, no evaluation will make sense. I personally feel that, if it is going to take you more than five to seven years to pay off that note, then in most cases, the practice evaluation may be too high. Keep in mind when evaluating the individual's tax return, in many cases, there are a lot of discrepancies that will allow you to have additional cash available to pay down notes. One discrepancy may be the owne's salary; it will decrease if he/she decides to work for you, and if no longer working for you. I would hope that that income would be available to you, providing you can maintain the same level of care and service or better.

In many cases, vacations, continuing education, car payments, miscellaneous expenses, insurance and pension plans and 401(k)s, dry cleaning, gas, food, and entertainment are run through small entities. However, if these expenses associated with the owner no longer apply because the owner is gone, that might create additional free cash to pay down notes. Be sure the appropriate professional evaluates these tax returns to make sure that this free cash is available to finance this debt.

The following list defines various investment terms that may provide information to you as you sit with your financial advisor and tax consultant to plan, not just your business investments, but your personal investments.

- Mutual funds are a package of stocks, bonds, or other instruments.
- A load is a sale fee that a mutual fund charges.
- A prospectus is a document describing objectives of operation and the risk of a particular fund.
- A trust is a legal document holding property on behalf of someone.
- A closed-end mutual fund issues shares only once and does not redeem shares unless the entire fund is liquidated.
- An open-ended mutual fund is always ready to issue new shares.
- ETF or exchange-traded funds were introduced in 1993. They are the second largest type of funds after open-ended mutual funds that invest in stocks, bonds, commodities, currency, and futures by combining features of stocks and mutual funds. The major disadvantage of an ETF is the cost of trading. ETFs could be more leveraged than a mutual fund. ETFs can be traded at any time that the market is open and an ETF offers more flexibility when it comes to accruing taxable income or capital gains.

With a short-term capital gain, you can sell the asset after holding that asset for less than one year; however, you are taxed as ordinary income. Long-term capital gains simply mean you are holding your asset longer than twelve months, and it will be generally taxed at a lower rate than ordinary income.

There are three classic stages in life and in business. Stage one generally involves hard work and creativity. Stage two is generally a period of stasis or maintaining the status quo. Stage three is a period of dispensation or loss. These stages are why so many businesses can go from rags to riches and back to rags.

The new investor thinks in twenty years or less, while the intermediate investor thinks in terms of around fifty years, and the long-term investor is thinking in terms of one hundred years. I strongly suggest that you contemplate creating a business that is dynamic and lasting. You want it to last and be passed on for the long term so that not only you, but also the parties that are employed after you, will continue to prosper.

You should consider the following four questions:

1. Is each member in your family and in your business thriving financially? If the answer is "no," you have some work to do.
2. Is the social impact among the members working and providing incentive? In other words, is your staff doing well personally and financially, and are the members of your family doing well? If the answer is "no," you have work to do.
3. Do the members of your family and the employees know how to leave your practice, but still choose not to? Are the conditions and the situations so good that there is no desire to relocate or leave?
4. Are the members of your family and in your employment meeting their responsibilities to manage their families and their businesses? Human, intellectual, and financial capital are the pillars to success, not only in your business endeavors, but also in your personal endeavors.

Most of us have little knowledge of investments and what the investments can do for us in the long term. What is investing really? It is spending your money, time, and other resources to create or acquire assets. An asset is anything that holds on to its value over time. The following will hopefully provide some information to stimulate you to study and inquire more about the power of proper investing.

There are four top threats to investments. They are market downturns, bankruptcy, inflation, and human nature. Really, what you are making is an investment in your future and in your life, so understanding these threats is important. There will always be market downturns, bankruptcy, inflation and the influences of human nature. So how do investors make money? By beating the market. Is this even possible? Can it actually be done? There are two schools of thought. First, The Efficient Market Hypothesis is a theory that suggests that the market fully incorporates information very quickly, whether this information is known or unknown. In the second theory, investors make money through material information, which is highly desirable and affects the market price of an asset. When this is revealed to the market, this private information is knowledge known to only a select few and generally this information is not shared. (Just as an aside, today stocks can trade on the market in less than 7/10,000 of a second. Eight years ago, a stock market trade took over ten seconds. This shows how quickly information is traded or shared.)

The wealth of the business is similar to the wealth of the family. It is made up of three central parts: human capital, intellectual capital, and financial capital. The human capital of the family is its members, and of the business, its employees and colleagues. Intellectual capital of the family is our experience and our knowledge that we pass on to children, and in business it is what the owner passes on to his or her associates. Financial capital in a family is what is in the bank, what is in our pockets. Financial capital in a business is the same; however, whether it is the receipt or the loss of financial capital, this surplus or lack of money will not necessarily lead to a happy/unhappy life. The financial capital is only a tool. It is only through the experienced generation, through the active enhancement of the younger generation's individual pursuits, that long-term wealth occurs in both business and in family which, in essence, is human capital. Keep in mind that for most of us, family, friends, colleagues, employees are the most important components of life.

In the end, I have always felt that life mimics business. There is a Chinese proverb that states, "...with money you can buy a house, but you cannot buy a home. You can buy a clock, but you cannot buy time. You can buy a bed, but not sleep. You can buy a book, but not knowledge. You can buy a doctor, but not health. You can buy a position, but not respect. You can buy sex, but not love." I think this message is important.

I hope you have enjoyed the above information and knowledge. Remember there is nothing you cannot accomplish, but it takes effort and hard work, and that is what makes it so special. It really is the journey, not the destination. **Best of luck!**

I would like to give credit below to individuals and books that have helped me develop my ideas over the years.

Bibliography

John C. Maxwell "The 21 Irrefutable Laws Of Leadership" Follow them and People Will Follow you

Professor Connel Fullenkamp "Understanding Investments"

Ms. Paulucci The SPECIAL Practice

Atty. Mark Cress

Mark Rosen CPA, CFP

Karen Noonan Interview Myths

John H. Fleming, Ph.D. and Jim Asplund Human Sigma Managing The Employee- Customer Encounter

Fred Reichheld The Ultimate Question

Jim Collins Good To Great

L. Ron Hubbard Speaking From Experience

Ken Blachard The Raving Fan

James E. Hughes Family Wealth Keep It In The Family

Becker Profession education Regulation

Taylor L. Coughlin CPA

Nina Coughlin for spending countless hours editing this book and organizing my ideas